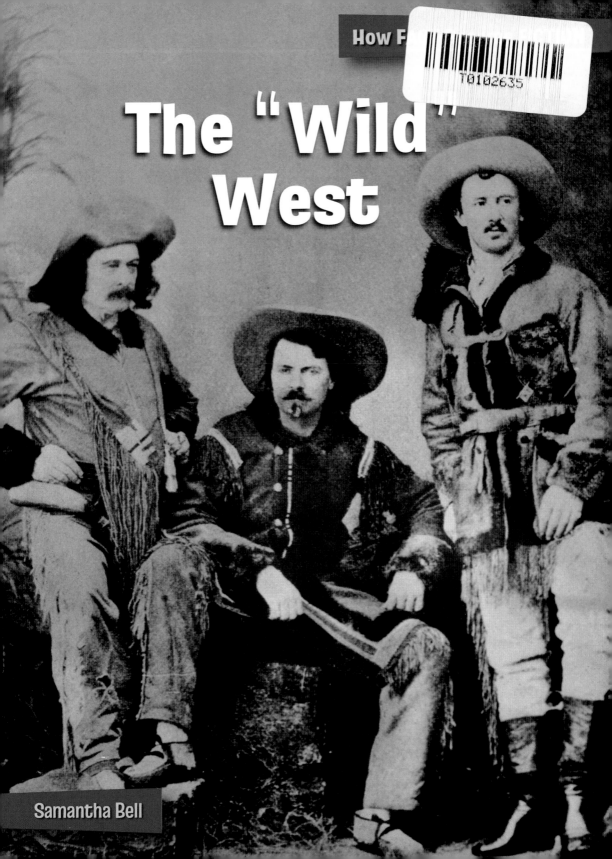

T0102635

The "Wild" West

Samantha Bell

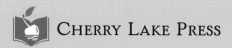

CHERRY LAKE PRESS

Published in the United States of America by Cherry Lake Publishing Group
Ann Arbor, Michigan
www.cherrylakepublishing.com

Reading Adviser: Beth Walker Gambro, MS, Ed., Reading Consultant, Yorkville, IL
Content Adviser: Heather Bruegl, M.A. (Oneida/Stockbridge-Munsee) Historian-Indigenous Consultant-Lecturer

Photo Credits: page 20: George Herbert Whitney/James M. Brown Collection, Library of Congress; page 21: Courier Litho. Co./Library of Congress; page 23: James W. Evans/The State Historical Society of Missouri; page 24: Helena Weekly Herald, 08 Dec. 1887/Chronicling America: Historic American Newspapers, Library of Congress; page 25: Boone County (Nebraska)/History Nebraska; page 26: Dakota tawaxitku kin, or, The Dakota Friend, 01 Oct. 1851/Chronicling America: Historic American Newspapers, Library of Congress; page 27: Chemung Valley Museum via Wikimedia Commons; page 28: Library of Congress; page 29: © Rena Schild/Shutterstock; page 30: © Stephen Orsillo/Shutterstock

Cherry Lake Press is an imprint of Cherry Lake Publishing Group.

Library of Congress Cataloging-in-Publication Data has been filed and is available at catalog.loc.gov.

Cherry Lake Publishing Group would like to acknowledge the work of the Partnership for 21st Century Learning, a Network of Battelle for Kids. Please visit http://www.battelleforkids.org/networks/p21 for more information.

Printed in the United States of America
Corporate Graphics

Note from publisher: Websites change regularly, and their future contents are outside of our control. Supervise children when conducting any recommended online searches for extended learning opportunities.

Samantha Bell was born and raised near Orlando, Florida. She grew up in a family of eight kids and all kinds of pets, including goats, chickens, cats, dogs, rabbits, horses, parakeets, hamsters, guinea pigs, a monkey, a raccoon, and a coatimundi. She now lives with her family in the foothills of the Blue Ridge Mountains, where she enjoys hiking, painting, and snuggling with their cats Pocket, Pebble, and Mr. Tree-Tree Triggers.

CONTENTS

CHAPTER 1

The Story People Tell

Adventure Awaits

There are stories people tell about the time when the United States expanded westward. Movies and television shows and even Disney attractions keep telling that story. It is a story about living on a **frontier**. On one side is civilization, with cities and roads and shops. On the other side is wilderness and lawlessness. That's what the story says anyway. In the story, the continent lay before American settlers heading west. The story calls that place the Wild West, or the Old West. It includes states west of the Mississippi River.

Cowboys are commonly part of stories about the Wild West.

In the story, the Wild West was a time and place marked by possibilities. For many Americans and even European immigrants, the West was a land of opportunity. Property, **bison**, and gold were abundant. Pioneers from the East built homesteads on free or cheap land granted by the U.S. government. Families who had nothing could build an American dream all their own.

The stories say this was also a time for adventure. Danger lurked in the Wild West. Cowboys drove cattle through raging rivers. Cowboys had to be tough. They rode hundreds of miles. They camped out under the stars. They carried guns and huddled around campfires at night. They'd ride

STRIKING IT RICH

There were many reasons the United States began expanding westward. One reason settlers moved west was for gold. When miners struck gold, newspapers across the country told everyone. The possibility of discovering gold brought about 300,000 migrants to the West. People came from around the world. They arrived on horseback, in covered wagons, and aboard ships. Miners also poured into Colorado, Idaho, Nevada, and Montana. Almost all of the miners were men. Whole towns popped up near gold mines. Once the mine was empty, many towns were abandoned.

Sheriffs were seen as protectors of the innocent in stories of the Wild West.

into town to gamble and drink. The stories made the life of a cowboy seem like a life of freedom.

The stories also say that **outlaws** made the West their home. Criminals robbed banks, stagecoaches, and carriages. People solved differences with shootouts in the street at high noon. Sheriffs, U.S. Marshals, and other law enforcement people were all that stood between innocent civilians and these bandits.

The stories of the Old West glorified the fight between the United States and Indigenous peoples, especially

Buffalo Bill's Wild West was a long-running show that capitalized on the well-worn tropes of "Cowboys and Indians" in the Wild West.

People who were not Native American found it fun to dress up as "Indians." Native Americans were seen as having one culture, and that culture became a novelty.

those of the **Great Plains.** The stories often showed Indigenous warriors attacking settlers and cowboys. They labeled Indigenous people as wild and savage. Children played "Cowboys and Indians," chasing each other with toy weapons. Indigenous peoples of the Great Plains were mocked. Their style of dress and way of life were reduced to costumes and misinformation.

Like with most stories, there is some truth in the tales of the Old West, but it wasn't as simple as the stories make it seem. Instead of a time of adventure, it was a time of conquest.

CHAPTER 2

The Facts of the Matter

Rapid Growth

European nations colonized North, South, and Central America for hundreds of years. The nations claimed areas of land. They ignored Indigenous claims on the land. European nations also traded this land with each other through treaties and purchases. As the colonies gained independence, the European land claims continued.

In 1803, President Thomas Jefferson bought a large area of land from France. It was called the Louisiana Purchase. It included 530 million acres (214.4 million hectares) of land from the Gulf of Mexico up across the Great Plains. The territory stretched west from the Mississippi River to the Rocky Mountains. Most European settlements were along the Mississippi River. New Orleans was the capital.

Thomas Jefferson was the third president of the United States from 1801 to 1809.

This map shows the area of land acquired by the Louisiana Purchase.

Indigenous peoples near European settlements in the Louisiana Purchase traded with colonists. Their way of life, and their independence, changed rapidly over the next 100 years.

The United States was already pushing farther west from the original 13 colonies. It claimed land in today's Ohio, Kentucky, and Tennessee. It sold the land to pay debts from the Revolutionary War. In the 1830s, the Indian Removal Act forced Indigenous peoples from the Eastern United States west across the Mississippi at gunpoint. In the 1840s, the Mexican-American War ended and the United States claimed more land in the South and Southwest, including California.

The United States sponsored **land rushes** to encourage American settlers to move west. Settlers came to mine, farm, and ranch. They were leaving a hard life behind. In the east, many of them lived in crowded, dirty cities. Their jobs did not pay enough. Children often went to work to help support the family. But in the West, people could become landowners.

DEATH OF THE BISON

When settlers first began to arrive, the West was home to massive herds of bison. About 30 to 60 million bison roamed from Canada all the way to Mexico. Most of them lived on the Great Plains. These herds were so big that the ground shook when the bison were on the move. From a distance, they sounded like thunder. Indigenous peoples had hunted the bison for thousands of years. Some nomadic peoples followed the herds. Others hunted them when the herds migrated to their area during the year. They used every part of the animal. They ate the meat. They made clothing from the hides, tools from the bones, and soap from the fat. No part of the bison was wasted.

But when the settlers came, the bison were killed by the thousands. Some people killed them for their hides. Tourists shot them for sport from the trains. U.S. soldiers killed the bison, too. By killing the bison, the soldiers took away the Native Americans' main food source. By the late 1880s, the bison were nearly gone.

In 1862, Congress passed the Homestead Act. Settlers could head west and get 160 acres (65 ha) of land the government claimed to own. They then built houses and barns on the land. They dug wells, plowed fields, and planted crops. After 5 years, they could apply to receive the official **title deed.** Hundreds of thousands of Americans used the Homestead Act to obtain land for free. Millions of acres of land went to western settlers. The completion of the railroads after the Civil War made traveling farther west easier. The U.S. Army defended settlers' claims. They drove Indigenous peoples off their homeland.

Vast amounts of land were used for raising cattle. The first cowboys were Spanish vaqueros. They managed herds of cattle as they rode on horseback. They were known for their exceptional roping, riding, and herding skills. Many English-speaking settlers who moved west

Vaqueros were known for their exceptional roping, riding, and herding skills.

followed the vaqueros' clothing style and methods of driving cattle.

When towns like Dodge City, Kansas, were first founded, gunfights and lawlessness took over for a short time. Danger was bad for business, though. Towns and cities quickly set up governments and police forces. Business and land development drove peace and prosperity. Still, some outlaws did take advantage of opportunities when they saw them. The most famous outlaws included Jesse James, Butch Cassidy, and Billy the Kid. Women could be outlaws, too. One of the most **notorious** was Belle Starr, also known as the "Bandit Queen."

CHAPTER 3

Spinning the Story

Eastern Entertainment

The lawlessness, adventure, and danger of the Wild West caught people's attention. Writers spun stories that exaggerated the danger. People were fascinated. William Cody started a traveling show. People could buy tickets to experience the adventure for themselves. The show was called Buffalo Bill's Wild West Show.

The idea for the show began with a writer named Edward Judson, also called Ned Buntline. Judson wrote small paperback books that sold for 10 cents each. These were known as dime-store novels. In 1869, Judson headed west to find inspiration for a new story. He met William "Buffalo Bill" Cody. Cody was a military scout and buffalo hunter. Judson wrote a dime-store novel about him. It was so popular that he wrote between 400 and 600 in all.

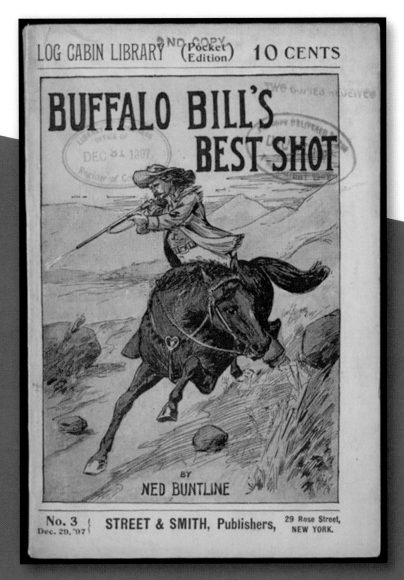

This is the cover of one of Ned Buntline's dime-store novels starring Buffalo Bill.

A photograph of Buffalo Bill Cody, star of
Buffalo Bill's Wild West Show.

Actors from *Buffalo Bill's Wild West Show* pose for a photograph.

Buffalo Bill Cody became famous around the country. Judson and Cody changed the story into a play, and eastern audiences loved it. Then in 1883, Cody had an idea. He decided to create a Wild West show. It would be an outdoor performance with cowboys, cowgirls, Native Americans, soldiers, horses, and bison.

The show was a hit. It was performed in cities around the country. There were trick horseback riders, ropers, and shooters. The show also included many wild animals.

In 1887, the show went on tour of Europe. It was so successful that Queen Victoria of Great Britain saw it three times.

Cody hired Indigenous people for the show. For a while, this included the famous Hunkpapa Lakota warrior Sitting Bull. The Lakota, along with many other nations, had been forced onto reservations. They were forced to be dependent on the U.S. government for food. They had no way to earn money for themselves. Cody paid Indigenous performers, but the show also made them act out **stereotypes**. They played the part of hostile warriors. They were presented as all the same, without their unique national identities.

A BIG CAST OF CHARACTERS

In the late 1890s, Buffalo Bill's show involved 500 cast and staff members. They included 25 cowboys, 12 cowgirls, and 100 Indigenous men, women, and children. They were all fed three hot meals every day. These were cooked on ranges that were 20 feet (6 meters) long. If they were staying in one place for a while, they lived in tents. Otherwise, they slept in railroad sleeping cars. The show generated its own electricity. It even had its own fire department.

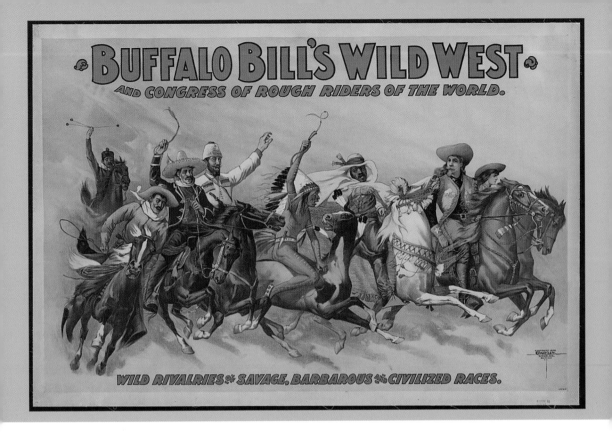

Buffalo Bill's shows had Indigenous actors play the part of brutal and unintelligent "savages." The way the show had actors dress and talk created stereotypes that still persist today.

Cody's show was not the only Wild West show to tour the country. It did so well that other shows soon followed. But it remained the largest and most successful. These false images of cowboys and Native Americans continued into the 20th century. The legend of the Wild West continued to grow. Movies, television shows, books, and music about the West became a large part of American entertainment.

CHAPTER 4

Writing History

Recognizing Bias

To understand what the period of western expansion was like, historians study sources from the time period. Many of these are firsthand accounts by the people who lived on the western frontier. They include letters, diaries, journals, and newspaper articles. These offer glimpses into the lives of those who wrote them.

When people moved to the West, they often left friends and family behind in the East. Letters were the only way they could communicate. Settlers wrote home about the things they saw and did. For example, a young man named John Howe settled in Wisconsin Territory in 1840.

James W. Evans wrote this letter to his brother in 1850. Evans traveled to California to mine gold. Here, he tells his brother not to come to California by land. He writes that he wouldn't cross the Great Plains again if someone paid him $25,000.00.

HELENA WEEKLY HERALD

Helena, Montana, Thursday, December 8, 1887.

The front page of Montana's *Helena Weekly Herald* from December 8, 1887, includes news about telegraph lines, fishing stories, jokes, and commentary.

In a letter to his parents in Vermont, he described how beautiful the land was. He told them how the prairies stretched as far as he could see. He told them about the wildlife he saw, including wolves, deer, and wild geese. He named the different types of fish that lived in the river. He talked about the cost of wheat, corn, and oats. Letters like this provide a picture of what life was like on the frontier.

Another type of source historians use to learn about the West are journals and diaries. These could include information about national events, local news, or the person's everyday life. For example, in 1868, a Texas cowboy named Jack Bailey kept a journal of his experiences on a cattle drive. The journal gave a firsthand account of his day-to-day activities. He included the ups and the downs of the drive as well as a few funny stories.

Newspaper articles are another good source of information. Western newspapers were printed either once a week or every day. Many times, they did more than just report the news. Some articles were about the land, plants,

CAPTURING THE MOMENT

Early photographic images became available in the 1840s and 1850s. Pioneer photographers traveled west to record the landscape and the people. They took photos of Indigenous peoples, buffalo hunters, and cowboys. Other photos featured outlaws, lawmen, and settlers. Some photo subjects were famous, while others were ordinary townspeople. These pictures show things that may be left out of a written record.

DAKOTA TAWAXITKU KIN

OR

THE DAKOTA FRIEND.

PUBLISHED MONTHLY BY THE DAKOTA MISSION.—G. H. POND, EDITOR.

VOL. I. ST. PAUL, MINNESOTA, OCTOBER, 1851. NO. 14.

MATTHEW CHAPTER 5.

43. Tuwe canteniciye cinhan, he canteyakiye kta, tuwe nicipajin kinhan, he yakipajin kta, eyapi ece qon he wanna nayaronpi.

44. Tuka mix heciciyapi, Tona nicipajinpi exta hena cantewicakiya po; qa tona niyaxicapi exta hena wicayawaxte po; qa tona niciyuxepi exta hena tantanyan ecawicakicon po; qa tona acanksiksiya nicuwapi exta hena cewicakiciciya po.

45. Hecen Ate yayapi, marpiya ekta yanke, cin he cinca niyanpi kta. Iye wi tawa on wicaxta xice wicaxta waxte ko aojanjan wicaya ece; qa oran owotanna qa oran owotanna xni ko *sakim* amagaju wicaya ece.

48. Hecen Ate yayapi, marpiya ekta yanke ecaca waxta kin he nix iyecen ecaca waxte po.

Iho, wicaxta xikxicaya cantekiciyuzapi qa xikxicaya okiciranyanpi kin, hena Wakantanka etanhan xni. "Tuwe tanyan cante makiyuze ca cantemakiye cinhan, he mix eya tanyan cante wakimduze ca cantewakiye kta; qa tuwe xicaya cante makiyuze, ca makiyuxe kinhan, he mix eya xicaya cante wakimduze ca wakimduxe kta," wicaxta apa ecinpi. Tokakiciyapi, xa kiciktepi, qa pa kiciyuzapi, qa yuha iwakicipi ece kin, he hetanhan icaga.

Owasin Wakantanka ate yapi keiciyapi tuka hececa. Iye hecen cante yuze xni, qa hecen ecaon wicaxi xni tuka. Toka exta cantekiye unxipi; qa tuwe xicaya taku ecaunkiconpi exta, itkom tanyan ecakicon unxipi. Wakantanka oran waxte kin he iwanyag unixipi, qa ecen econ unxipi Tuwe econ qa Wakantanka ate ya keye cinhan, he wicake kta. Owasin econpi unkanx wicowaxte kta tuka.

Dakota and English.

Dakota apa tatanka ecedan wacinyanpi.
The buffalo is the whole dependence of some of the Dakotas.

Waziyata ta ota keyapi.
It is said that there are many in use to the north.

Dakota wanjikxi tarinca nom qinpi okihipi.
A few Dakotas can carry each two deer at a time.

Dakota xonka ota wicayuhapi.
The Dakotas keep a great many dogs.

Xonktokeca xongidan ko ota,
Wolves and dogs are plenty.

Xonktanka akan wicayotankapi ece.
Horses are used to ride on.

Apa waranksica ito cekiyapi hehan kutepi.
Some first pray to the bear and then shoot him.

Mato ote terika keyapi.
It is said that the grizzly bear is hard to to kill.

Magatanka, maga magaxekxecadan ko gaksica ko ota.
Swan, geese brant and ducks are plenty.

Capa, ptan, napagica, skeca, dokxica, sinkpe ko, hena hanyaqeepi on he wicaxta zapi.
The skins of the beaver, otter, marten, fisher, mink, and muskrat are taken for the fur.

Dakota woteca odepi eca, wotihnapi eca pi ece; qa watutka odepi eca, wakute eyapi; qa takut owasin odepi eca, wahnapi eyayi eca.
When the Dakotas hunt large animals (as deer,) they call it *hunting food*; when they hunt only small animals, they call it *shooting*; and when they hunt any and every thing, they simply call it *hunting*.

It will be observed in this lesson, that the names of the buffalo and the deer are derived from that of the moose; the names of the horse, wolf, and fox, from that of the dog; and the names of the swan, brant, and duck from that of the goose.

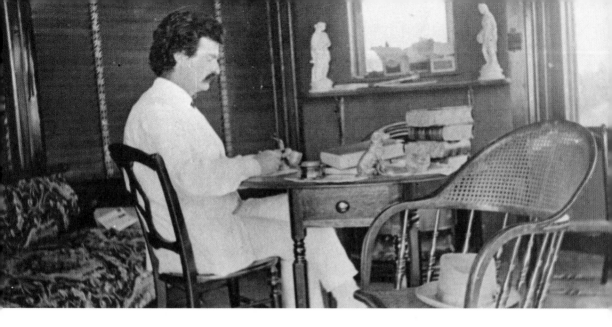

Samuel Clemens first used his famous pen name, Mark Twain, while a frontier journalist in Nevada in the early 1860s.

and farming. Journalists also wrote about religion, politics, court cases, and Indigenous relations. A few newspapers were printed by and for Indigenous nations themselves. For example, in the early 1850s, *The Dakota Friend* was published in Minnesota in both the Dakota language and in English. The articles included news about the Dakota people, retellings of Dakota history, and news on government treaties.

All of these sources contain a point of view. Sometimes that point of view included **bias**. Bias is an idea for or against something. It is usually not based on fact. It can be unfair. The bias at the time was the idea that

The Hunkpapa Lakota chief, Sitting Bull (left), traveled with Buffalo Bill's show. He gave speeches to gather support for Indigenous issues.

Indigenous peoples were savage and "wild." Many people believed that Indigenous people did not deserve to live. They thought they were in the way of America's right to the land. Even the term "Wild West" shows this bias. People at the time believed that European civilization was the only way to live. They did not respect the complex lives, social structure, and civic organization of Indigenous peoples.

Indigenous peoples are still fighting this bias today. The stories and stereotypes that dominated westward expansion continue today. Luckily, progress is being made to right some of the wrongs of the past. Indigenous peoples like the Lakota work to reclaim some of what was lost. Language and cultural programs help to preserve the many different identities and cultures indigenous to North America.

When investigating history, it is important to look for bias. Ask questions about people's opinions and why they have them. Are those opinions based on fact? Are they fair? Look for information from multiple perspectives. Find out what other people thought and why. This is how you can help separate fact from fiction.

Activity

A Day in the Life

One way historians discovered the true story of the Wild West is by reading journals that people wrote. Many journals recorded everyday activities. Create a journal entry about your day. Think through the day and write down what you did. You can also write down how you felt. Your journal entry does not have to be exciting. It is a record of the day's events and what you thought of them.

Learn More

Books

Cooke, Tim. *Go West with Cowboys and Ranchers.* New York, NY: Crabtree Publishing Company, 2016.

Edelstein, Robert. *Legends of the Wild West: True Tales of Rebels and Heroes.* New York, NY: Centennial Books, 2020.

Pascal, Janet. *What Was the Wild West?* New York, NY: Penguin Workshop, 2017.

Smith, James Otis. *Black Heroes of the Wild West.* New York, NY: Toon Books, 2020.

On the Web

With an adult, explore more online with these suggested searches.

Buffalo Bill Center of the West

"Buffalo Bill Cody," America's Story

Museums of Western Colorado

The Wild West

Glossary

bias (BYE-uhs) an opinion or presentation of facts that is unfairly for or against something or someone

bison (BY-suhn) a very large mammal with a big head, humped shoulders, and short curved horns

frontier (fruhn-TEER) an area that marks the edge of settled or colonized land

Great Plains (GRAYT PLAYNZ) a broad stretch of flatland in North America located west of the Mississippi River and east of the Rocky Mountains

land rushes (LAND RUHSH-uhs) opening of land for homesteading based on first arrival; people would line up at the border and race to claim land

notorious (noh-TOR-ee-uhss) known for something bad

outlaws (OWT-lawz) someone running away from the law or living in illegal ways

stereotypes (STAIR-ee-uh-tyeps) a simplified idea about a group that is usually untrue or only partially true and is often harmful and insulting

title deed (TY-tuhl DEED) a legal document that transfers ownership of property from one person to another

Index